FINISHING LINE PRESS

www.finishinglinepress.com

HOMESCAPES

poems by

Lee Woodman

Finishing Line Press
Georgetown, Kentucky

HOMESCAPES

ACKNOWLEDGMENTS

My great appreciation to Donna Baier Stein, Editor, and Lisa Sawyer,
Managing Editor, of Tiferet Journal, where poems in this book, sometimes
in earlier versions, first appeared:

"Father's Roll top"
"Trees Have Longer Lives"
"Understood Pasts, Untold Futures"
"Visit to Varanasi Forty-Seven Years Later"
"Waiting on the Wall in Delhi"

And to Annemarie Lockhart, Founding Editor, and Nathan Gunter,
Managing Editor, of vox poetica for publishing:

"A Mulch Pile Prayer"
"Betula Papyrifera"

Also to Diane Smith of Grey Sparrow Press for publishing:

"Road Trip to Nilokheri"
"Jaya the Ayah"

Publisher: Leah Maines
Editor: Christen Kincaid
Cover Art: Lee Woodman
Author Photo: Sonya Melescu
Cover Design: Elizabeth Maines McCleavy

Printed in the USA on acid-free paper.
Order online: www.finishinglinepress.com
        also available on amazon.com

Author inquiries and mail orders:
Finishing Line Press
P. O. Box 1626
Georgetown, Kentucky 40324
U. S. A.

Table of Contents

INDIA

Road Trip to Nilokheri 1
Murder at Nizamuddin..3
Two Dinners at Eight 4
Tommy at the American Embassy, New Delhi.............................5
Jaya the Ayah..6
A Pillowy Bosom 7
Rolling Socks with Jacob John at Edward Elliot Road................9
Waiting on the Wall in Delhi 11
First Bike..13
Home Leave...14
Dancing at the Ashoka Hotel 15
His Holiness 17
Climbing the Rohtang Pass 18

AMERICA

Coming Home to New Hampshire 21
Homeroom Ghazal..22
Summer Prelude 23
Afternoon Traditions 24
Betula Papyrifera 25
Old Time Fair, New Hampshire 26
Weekly Flea 27
Trees have Longer Lives...28
Father's Roll Top 30
End of Season..32
Benumbed 33
A Mulch Pile Prayer 34
Found in a New Hampshire Cottage 36

STEREOSCOPE

Ruby Necklace...41
Understood Pasts, Untold Futures 42
Family Cabin...43
Can My Two American Homes Relate? I Eavesdrop...................45

Snowporch...47
I Wish I Had Asked More about Priscilla...................................48
From the High Shelf...50
Nursing Home in New London, NH 52
Visit to Varanasi Forty-Seven Years Later 54
Homescapes...55
Thanks..57

for Betsy

INDIA

Road Trip to Nilokheri

A hundred blistering kilometers from home,
we bump along the rutted road to Nilokheri.
My Dad hums above the diesel's drone,
I am proud to travel with him.

We chat during these trips, taking note of
particular colors in the trees—emerald,
jade, sage. We compare baseball
to ballet—warm-ups, footwork, sore muscles.

A warm wind blows, the dust rises.
Through sooty windows, I detect wobbling air.
Ripples of cool from the nullah's water
battle currents of heat that flare down.

A water buffalo sinks into the gully mud,
flat trapezoidal nose barely above the surface.
Long lashes bent downward, he blinks,
shakes flies buzzing at his ears.

School children, sent outside to the yard
make way for teachers from neighboring districts.
These men, wearing white dhotis
and cracked brown sandals, wait at sagging tables.

Women drape a burlap banner to cover
peeling patches on the whitewashed plaster wall.
"W-e-l-c-o-m-e, honored speaker." I sound out
curly Hindi letters, painted dark purple.

Dad offers me a drink from the ice chest
we pulled from the trunk—"Coming with me?"
Settled on the cooler, drinking Coca Cola
from its green glass bottle, I shake my head.

I stay back, as a slender villager
draped in orange-red sari, lemon-chiffon shawl,

gives small metal plates of food to children.
Folding smoky chapatis, they scoop rice and dahl.

After lunch, the children call to me,
"Come deeti, come!"
Barefoot, they scuff the ball across a rough
path toward the car—I slip off the chest.

Playmates giggle as I fumble the ball.
High in the kikar tree, a mynah bird jeers.
Sparrows perched on lower branches scatter
at the clang of dirty plates.

At sundown, teachers follow Dad to the car.
I help him flip the cooler to lighten the weight,
slushy water dribbles away on bone-dry ground.
Only one coke and a cucumber remain.

He starts the motor. Village elders
salaam, pressing palms together—Namaste.
Sputtering back to the main road, we
begin the trek toward the roadside rest house.

We talk about typical *dak* bungalows—
dirty stucco, russet trim. We can picture
the spare rooms—single dangling lightbulb,
jute string charpoys. Still, we will sleep well.

The journey is tiring. Truck caravans tie up roads,
crowds surround an injured cow by the wayside.
But the durwan's greeting is warm, he promises
treats for the morning—soft boiled eggs, oat toast.

A weak trickle from the shower is sublime.
Hungry, we taste our surviving cucumber—
melony, slightly sweet, faintly salty—
the last warm coke, delicious.

Murder at Nizamuddin

I stood
by the pond,
dark water camouflaged by tall leafy plants

Sturdy
pink blossoms,
anchored among tough tuberous roots, shot skyward

A little boy
about my age
waited for the frog's throat to bulge, its eyes

to swivel atop
its knobby head.
He swatted full force with a broken cricket bat

Stillness
A flat-out hush as
water pooled in the shallow bowl of foliage

I never told
our bearer,
Gurkha Ram, where I had been that morning

At naptime
he carved
a row of teak elephants, linking trunks to tails

Toward twilight
he held my hand
as we stepped carefully around a small red ant

making its way to the pond.
He showed me
how the lotuses were looking after the dragonflies

Two Dinners at Eight

Double doors. The concave screen—a damp sieve.
I enter.
Ice cubes clinking, both sides of their room,
whiskey and soda on the shiny black dresser,
mother sitting before the mirror.
Whiskey and soda on the matching lacquered bedside table,
father propped up on wrinkled sheets reading *The Herald*.
I climb over him and lie at his side.
A yellowed fan circles above,
the black dot of paint on the blade comes around and around.
She twirls in silver purple taffeta,
spinning perfumed breezes from her scalloped skirt.
Bougainvillea branches press
against three tall windows casting
spears of shadows into the room.
A car idles in the driveway below, a turbaned driver waits.
My parents won't be at dinner downstairs tonight,
older sister at boarding school, little sisters with the ayah.
I'll sit at the head of the table, legs swinging metronome-style.
A bearer will stand by silently and
last night's boiled pudding will be this night's steam-fried.

Tommy at the American Embassy, New Delhi

Sixth grade.

Shocked, I tasted the sweet escaping honey of
     your mouth.

That night,

I conjured your face close to my pillow,
     concentric curl in the middle of your
          forehead.

Locked alone behind the bathroom door,
     I re-read your note:

Perfectly round-shaped letters,
     three sheets of lined paper folded
          over and over and over.

Privately thrilled, publicly shy,

I stepped close to the bench while
     you were up at bat, cap over curl.

I blushed and heard them whisper,
     "That's Tommy's girl."

Jaya the Ayah

Dark oiled hair pulled severe in a low bun,
she smelled of vinegar. We hated the garlic
she fried, burnt red chilies seemed sinister.

She braided our sister's hair too tight,
beat us with an old slipper—worn nail heads
sticking out of the sole.

I feared her evil threat to lock me
in the bathroom and dangle red chilies
across my bare labia lips.

Once she came out of there and I cringed as
pink blood, filled with black crimson leeches,
swirled down the commode.

The day her boyfriend cycled by,
our parents finally acknowledged her venom.
Jaya burst toward him cursing with spit,

took his arm, her jaw clenched hard,
Snap! She broke his bone in two.
He shrieked in disbelief.

Mother drew us together to say Jaya was fired.
Who had lit the match?
Terror-struck, our cheeks red-hot,

we imagined searing flames, horrified to think
she still lay burning on her pyre.

A Pillowy Bosom

Church Park Convent School,
Madras, India.
Cross-legged under
trees, we chanted
multiplication tables.

Nuns wearing
black and white
starched tunics,
taught us
sums and grammar,
their
fleshy chins,
wrapped in cowls.

I presumed
they were stern,
wondered how
they slept or ate
or if they
put their toes
into the ocean
at Edward Elliot Beach.

The day
I fell off
the jungle gym,
a Sister rushed
to rescue me.
Her underskirts swirled
above my head—
pink underpants!

She scooped me up,
sweetly squashed me
to her chest—
soft flowery poitrine

scented with linen
perfume—
Her name so gentle,
Sister Carmel.

Rolling Socks with Jacob John at Edward Elliot Road

The dhobi rode his bike up the driveway,
teetering, piled laundry stacked on back.

Everything neatly pressed and folded
for the bearer's approval—except the socks.

Old Jacob John was always ready, and I
was too. We had skilled labor to perform.

Gathering all the pairs, we'd kneel
comfortably near the dining room table.

He'd demonstrate rolling technique,
coaching in his Tamil-English cadence,

"Toe to toe, heel to heel, Lilli Baba,
all smooth, all must be smooth."

I admired his dark umber hands deftly
rolling toes to heels and all the way up.

Pure magic the way he took the lip
of one sock and wrapped it around the roll.

Perfection. We admired our handicraft—
colorful rows of completed sock-balls,

lined up carefully along the low footboard
before we carried them off to cupboards.

Jacob John, majordomo of our household,
supervised everything—tasted the curry,

inspected the marigolds, tracked expenses,
adapted to quirks of the Memsahib.

To me he was a genius—even guessed
where my pet Star would birth her babies

atop the bookshelf behind my bed. There they
were, fur balls tucked into a jigsaw frame,

her multicolored kittens, all in tidy rolls—
not so different from the socks.

Waiting on the Wall in Delhi

9 AM
I clamber up the courtyard's brick wall,
feet finding toe-holds in the crumbling mortar.
Settled astride the top ledge, a flat perch, I have a perfect
lookout along the roadway from 34 Nizamuddin East.

10 AM
Tall trees drape over the wall, bending toward burnt grass
on the house side, dropping dried leaves and faint blooms
along the roadside. I pull long white beans from the khejdi tree,
blow dandelion puffs from their supporting twigs.

11 AM
Nigel and Gillian are to arrive this morning. I picture
their car packed with faded brown cases, a tin of biscuits.
Most likely they will come by Ring Road, passing
Humayan's Tomb. All moves too slowly, a silent Saturday.

NOON
A pye-dog sniffs along the roadway as a white spot near
his neck rides lazily up and down his bony shoulder.
He slinks forward, headed toward the empty park,
where a parakeet and a black crow peck berries.

1 PM
The day half gone, the wind grows warmer.
Two swaying ladies carry large shallow baskets balanced
on their heads. I squint at neatly stacked dung
cakes that send up whiffs of syrupy charred odor.

2 PM
Sad that my friends are going to leave the country,
I count only a few hours left before their flight.
A hopeful rumble of a battered taxi passes,
two tiny brass gods swinging from its rear-view mirror.

3 PM
A green rickshaw follows, carrying a young boy with black eyes.
His thin father pedals the cycle with difficulty. The child sits
backwards on the hard bench, crowded by piles of
aluminum tins and cups they are taking to the bazaar.

4 PM
Long branches of the peelu tree bow more slowly,
the breeze has stilled, another black crow caws in the distance.
A horn beeps rudely! Time disappears.
I'll pretend I just got here when they come to the gate.

First Bike

I called her   "Ofeelya Bumps"
      loose steering,   deep grooved treads,
          zig-zagged   tossed gravel

Our old neighborhood   Chanakyapuri,
          residential,
     We'd venture out   unsupervised

Hey, MaryAnn!   We used to snack
      on Velveeta cheese   smeared with ketchup,
         mustard   before riding

Remember the rabid dog?   Torn ear
      running jaggedly,   crooked mouth,
         saliva   dripping

I swerved those red wheels back and forth   To
      dizzy him.   I prayed
        through heartbeats

Thick handlebars   fat tires   How far is the gate?
     please   please
        be there to open

Home Leave

What should I answer? How to explain?
Do you really go to school in New Delhi?
We were curious strangers both home and away.

Three months of questions, some hard to convey
Do you speak Hindu? Do you wear saris?
What should I answer? How to explain?

Do you ride elephants? Been to Bombay?
Do you eat curry? What is a lychee?
We were curious strangers both home and away.

What are you doing in the U.S.A?
Do you like TV? Know how to ski?
What should I answer? How to explain?

"We're visiting family. Dad's on holiday.
We love Grandma's ice cream. We're glued to TV!"
We were curious strangers both home and away.

On return to New Delhi, my friends will all say,
Where were you during the Lights of Diwali?
How should I answer? How to explain?
We were curious strangers both home and away.

Dancing at the Ashoka Hotel

Matching crinoline dresses
suggested we were twins

She was more than thirty,
I was less than ten

Scruffy loft, downtown Delhi,
Mom built a school for ballet

Wooden floors, crooked barres,
piano, hardly Steinway

The troupe she trained, quite motley,
we hoped someday to shine

Tchaikovsky kept us moving,
out loud, she counted time

A young man came from Broadway,
traveled eastward on his own

He heard a spunky lady
brought western dance to town

Such a novel pairing—
gay Richard and my Mom

They danced in hotel nightclubs,
a sprite and the grande-dame

Dad's surviving photos show
Richard sporting stripey vests

Leading Mom through Polish polkas,
they twirled among the guests

Once I was invited
to dance along beside them

I tripleted and do-see-doed and
waltzed with six-foot patrons

As flower girl, my dress was blue,
embroidered with pink roses

Colored ribbons crowned my hair,
a huge bouquet of posies

Mom would point her toe and smile,
full of joie-de-vivre

I'd tip my hat, the broad-rimmed one,
and dream that I were she

His Holiness

Palms up, arms outstretched, we walk slowly toward Him.
Our private audience, June 1959.
Draped over Dad's forearms, a white silk scarf, the khata.

He transfers the garment to the Dalai Lama's arms,
I fix on the Leader's slim brown body, loose garnet robe,
smallpox vaccination, thick-framed black eyeglasses.

He asks about my father's religion, his work,
why he is in India. Sonam Topgai, interpreter, helps
Dad comprehend His Holiness's escape from Tibet.

He leads us to the children's encampment by the river—
no beds, heat from small charcoal fires and twigs,
a ball of fried dough morning and evening, tin cups of tea.

My father films the Dalai Lama's sister who's in charge,
and inquires of her helpers, "What do you need?"
They don't say food, clothes, blankets, or water, only

 "Could you send us a teacher?"

Cleaning the attic, I found the folder, "Dalai Lama."
Yellowed letters from Dad to Sonam Topgai,
accounts of another visit with His Holiness in America.

The still-exiled Leader of Tibet spoke at Harvard in 1980.
Security guards balked as my father set up an old projector
to show flickering films of rosy-cheeked children by the river.

Unconcerned, the Dalai Lama entered the receiving room.
As the footage rolled, he shot off his divan, jumped forward
to touch the screen images of his beloved late sister.

His Holiness motioned his assistant to bring a silk khata,
draped it over Dad's outstretched arms. Sweet silence—
his gesture of protection. No words, a sole beatific smile.

Climbing the Rohtang Pass

Barely twelve, I understood how daunting the climb:
Rohtang Pass, Himachal Pradesh, border of India.

Elevation—thirteen thousand, a three-day ascent—
Stay-over at two base camps, canvas tents, oolong tea.

Small trekking party with mules and supplies; practiced
sherpas scanning for snow, deadly landslides.

Difficult terrain to the south, Kullu Valley, forests of deodar;
rocky rubble to the north, Spiti Valley, jagged peaks.

Throughout the years, those who chanced the crossing
learned that Rohtang Pass meant "Pile of Corpses."

The Gods' Mountain jealously guarded that name;
human beings attempting to change it were met with silence.

Dad's photo of me when I reached the Pass, stretching
out prone on top—corduroy pants, wooly jacket, Tibetan cap.

I felt airborne into China, hovering over mounds of ice.
Perhaps those frozen souls below had chosen to stay there.

The rush of wind, vast endless view could drown us all—
a sensation of snow under our bellies for the rest of time.

AMERICA

Coming Home to New Hampshire

You, Madras, with shimmering mica in your sea,
wooden boats smelling of salt and fish.
Sister Carmel taught me to read under trees.
At four, I rode a rickshaw home to Edward Elliot Road.

You, Delhi, where we washed our hands with Dettol,
soft ladies wore red saris and large cut diamonds.
Jeti brushed my hair with coconut oil.
At eight, I rode my bike to school through Rashtrapati Bhavan.

You, New Hampshire, your fresh white milk and bracing air,
kids at New London High School wore penny loafers.
Homeroom teacher, Mr. Morris, introduced me as the new kid,
"She must mean Indiana." Ashamed, I walked down Main Street.

Homeroom Ghazal

Not long ago, India was my home, now it would be America,
but home is a relative word.

They said I'd be in sophomore homeroom, what did that mean?
Could home be a room? Could a room be a home?

Placed in junior French and freshman math, was I a sophomore?
Was home where you were or who you were?

My teacher said I had a British accent; everyone spoke English
with New Hampshire accents, but America was their homeland.

I wore lightweight dresses and thin glass bangles, wrist to elbow.
Only snow boots would do in this hometown, New London.

Easy to find churches up and down Main Street, but temples?
Mosques? No small "g" gods or goddesses, not in this home state.

Everything was big—the roads, cars, girls with significant breasts.
How do you make yourself at home?

Come springtime, Bobby Garrett invited me to a sock hop—
sock? hop? American Bandstand helped me prepare at home.

From Boston, WBZ played songs I had heard on Radio Ceylon:
"Great Balls of Fire", "Twist and Shout"—now I felt at home.

Glued to our first-time-ever TV, Mom would be immersed in
"As the World Turns" when I got home. Indeed, it was turning.

Summer Prelude

Fierce windstorm visited last night,
    a formidable gale intending to stay.

Bolt of lightning came all too near,
    hammering forth a flooding rain.

Screen porch began to collapse,
    dented plastic table scudded across wooden planks,
        cowered near the sliding glass door.

Deck chairs tipped over face down, legs up,
            dinner plates sprayed.

Prosecco bottles rolled, showering the floor.

Afternoon Traditions

Steamy August. Ragged Mountain Road.
We three, two sisters and a cousin,
head down the rutted gravel path to Cole Pond.
Cold! pond, ringed by deep green pines,
a birch or two, a crimson swamp maple.

We girls know the plan.
Snap the annual photo standing by the dock,
same bathing suits, different colors.
We'll shed them to skinnydip
as soon as we reach the raft.

We single-file across cement slabs,
over the narrow bridge, above a rushing brook.
Sprays of 4-foot orange day lilies
touch our forearms. We eye how high
the water line climbs up the diving rock.

Shrill squeals as we brace
for the cold shock at our waists.
We flip on our backs to bob silently,
velvety water circles our thighs. Cicadas chirp
as our 5 o'clock loon dives for his trout.

Betula Papyrifera

I've never known the names of trees before,
        whereas you, I commit to memory.

"White Lady of the Woods" for some,
        in India, they call you "Burgha."

Your slender twigs chase old spirits away,
        inviting me to enter.

At my peril, I will nestle
        near the myrrh of your arm,

brushing the fragrance,
        smoothing the oil of acer.

I'll mingle my voice, join the rustling
        of your leaves,

and murmur susurrus,
        "Come lie with me on mossy beds."

The breeze carries pollen, resins keep our blood hot,
        fallen needles beckon our embrace.

You are my magic spell, the graceful tree
        I've learned to write on.

Old Time Fair, New Hampshire

A country fair
and crowd—
Street sign punches the sky,
letters
in lilac on
white tin,
floating
high,
un-noticed
by busy
villagers
with ice cream cones—
Village of Cilleyville.

Chocolate dripping
off chins,
Young guys pumping handcars
ogle cute
senior girls
riding their
"One-wheelers."
The boys sigh
knowing these
cool chicks
with wire-frame specs
will be gone next fall.

Weekly Flea

The Flea claimed *Shopper-classified,*
in biz since '93—
bridging gap for buyers/sellers.
Did not convince me.

An ad for sweater dryer, marked
$5, *prevents shrinking—*
fits over tub, raised airflow too,
I stopped and started thinking…

What did it cost to place that ad?
What about the others?
Women's sneakers, worn just once,
Christian cassettes, $10.

Blankets, horses, small and large,
oak barrels—heavy duty.
Bisexual man for 'some fun times'
King mattress, 'Call Bev Wednesday.'

Antique woodworking tools, and more:
Vintage doors, old bottles—
Drivers side-mirror off old
Suburban, iron grill for waffles!

I thought about that sweater dryer,
Asked about it twice—
OBRO, or best reasonable offer,
some wiggle room in price.

Trees have Longer Lives

I know the voluminous Hemlock on my mountain

will always know more than I.

Tall, erect, it once stood alongside young hedges that since surrendered.

Over years, the giant sent long roots below— not to harm anything, only to stand strong.

Many trees huddle amidst families,

this one remains alone.

What we pass fleetingly, the wizened one protects:

boisterous bickering of blue jays and squirrels;

black bear with brown muzzles, growing fur for the season;

Siberius Iris, bursting perfume through raindrops;

overjoyed children, galloping with laughter;

sad conversations between lovers no longer.

The Hemlock absorbs all life's events:

attacks endured, sun saluted, sorrows sustained.

Its supple trunk carries the load, leaves clapping their memories.

I hope never to witness rings or scars,

but to revel in its graceful branches reaching ever higher, blowing us messages.

For my revered tree will have longer thoughts than we, and

longer longings.

Father's Roll Top

Pulling faded limp trousers off the night hook
with the help of a taped-up walking stick,
he rocks unsteadily to his desk, stretch socks
hugging fat ankles.
He clutches the writing surface with swollen hands,
one misshapen, missing the tip of a thumb.

Lifting the scarred roll top,
he pulls out stacks of papers
from beneath rows of tiny drawers,
and eases down slowly.
He trusts the burgundy leather chair with steel casters
will receive his sluggish weight.

He leans towards the nearby window,
and contemplates the hillside.
A red suspender slips off his shoulder,
scraping loose spackle and cracked chips
from much-painted frames.

An Old Boston pencil sharpener nailed to the sill
offers up its roundabout of multi-sized holes,
but the handle is rusty.
He glares at the blank page,
swears when the pencil breaks again,
sweeps the paper stack away.

Until a flock of purple finches,
swoop in, hopping and screeching,
forcing him to take measure.
This, too, is their homeland
where they search for seeds among
primrose and wild strawberries.

Warbling loudly, they alight with a whoosh
headed for the hemlock that offers him shade.
Slowly he bends for his pen,

heartened by kinsmen aligned on a branch.
He scratches out, *"Navy airman Robbie raced…"*
Finches, too, have written their stories—
Quills, tipped in raspberry, leave timeless marks.

End of Season

Last morning two brittle black crickets

lay upside down inside the doorway.

Last night the mourning dove slowed its moan.

Last swim at dusk—shadows rippled

over the green mountain,

a single car rumbled across gravel.

Two early trees turn red in the meadow,

two large black bees hover in and out,

but don't find what they need.

The hydrangea bush, so stalwart all summer—

its shriveling blossoms wrestle to stay white.

Benumbed

It can get dark on the mountain
A faint sun without hope disappears,
you are surrounded by silence

Hollow trees have already
wrapped their arms around
themselves

A slash of thin leaves provides
no home for the lone bear who
circles the frozen ground

Rare flashes from stars reflect
birds frozen mid-air, iced by
stinging winds

A moose with heavy antlers
backs away from the lake,
dead otters line the creek

Determined spiders crawl slowly
up your torso to pull
your eyelids shut

A dull ache cups your ears,
the band tightening around your head
It can get dark on the mountain

A Mulch Pile Prayer

Our Father who art in the mulch pile,
Hallowed be thy Brussels sprouts.

I embroidered this on a placemat
I knew would make him chuckle.

Thy corn has come, thy will was done,
on earth as it was on the sunporch.

He hung it above his desk with delight,
proud of my inherited irreverence.

Third generation Unitarian,
staunch, puritanical, though wily in speech:

"Holey Cleist!" he'd squeal, "what
the hell is the Holey Ghost?"

Give us this day, our daily tomates,
and deliver us from Swiss chard.

He was proud of his fruits and roots,
sweet "bluebs" and rutabagas—

He'd plea with us to weed with him;
I'd skitter off after two hard tugs.

Although he could rototill no more,
he'd stoop with aching joints and pull,

Shaking loose rich mulch from carrots,
praising lush abundant squash.

Lead us not!

into his garden that neighbors
turned into pretty flowers.

I'm glad he never saw the field of
day lilies overtake his asparagus.

He confessed once before he died
he and Mom recited the Lord's Prayer,

every night holding hands in bed,
tending the earth again under starry sky.

Beneath those beets and lettuce leaves,
he planted his brand of bountiful faith.

I sent a joyful message skyward,
sailing right past pews of red zinnias:

*For thine is the power and the most glorious green
thumb forever...Amen.*

Found in a New Hampshire Cottage

We own this home, but he left clues—
a duffel bag, love letters.
His sturdy revolver in a trunk,
deep among the clutter.

I still smell piss under the shrubs,
outside his basement den,
his hips too frail to climb the steps
to reach upstairs again.

In France, he had to pee in foxholes,
standing watch along the shore.
As an old man in this cottage,
he waged another war.

We found a few Moroccan rugs,
years of memorabilia.
Hindu gods held court atop
Asian rosewood furniture.

My mother left some Degas prints,
brass lamps from Anatolia.
He kept his memories downstairs,
the cliffs and shores of Omaha.

A workshop meant for tools and brooms
became a war museum.
Photos, maps, old newspapers,
yellowed in memoriam.

Headlines screamed out "Normandy!"
echoed by shrieks at nighttime.
He relived blasts of heads shot off,
deafened for a lifetime.

The metal "cricket" on his bench,
in wartime signaled friend or foe,

click once to identify yourself,
pray for two clicks, then you knew.

Years later, there still is an urn
we plan to bury sometime.
Silent ashes, near the clicker,
rest against two fists of twine.

STEREOSCOPE

Ruby Necklace

Sixty years ago, jeweler Nanda Lal Varma
    Pedaled to our front door, Chanakyapuri, New Delhi
    Laid a black velvet cloth on the living room rug
    Spilled a bag of precious stones, started his sketch—

Heart-shaped gold filigree tree, curlicues of branches and leaves
    Decked with regal red birds, splashing crystal water
    A lacey breastplate studded with rubies, diamonds, pearls—
    the heirloom necklace my Mom left to me.

I wore it to the Kennedy Center not long ago, rubies cascading
Down the deep décolletage of my green silk dress,
    Pearls spreading across frosted gold branches,
    Diamonds aglow, I was almost—

Mom,
    Floating into Covent Garden for the opening of Swan Lake
    Toasting with champagne at the Ambassador's State dinner
    Waltzing with Iqbal Singh at the Delhi Golf Club Gala Ball

As the conductor swept up his baton for the finale of Turandot
    Chandeliers sprayed showers of diamonds across the orchestra
    Red velvet chairs rose in perfect harmony above the Box Circle
    Guests twirled upward in corkscrew turns from the balcony

For a moment, the world was in unison, floating
    Nanda Lal Varma cycled by, bike streamers riffling
    Scarlet birds sparkled, iridescent leaves shimmered
    I felt a gentle tap on my sternum as I lifted my arms—

Mom's reminder to keep my shoulders back and head high
    My first ballet teacher, she was exacting about port-de-bras
    First one to take me to the Opera too. Smiling, she bowed—
    Playing to the gallery right through the skylights

Understood Pasts, Untold Futures

I see you through the glass door,
       as you come down the hillside covered with grass,
          down brick steps to my cottage.

A splintered wooden handrail guides you past juniper,
       surrounded by moss phlox
          that bloomed in the spring.

You spot me through the glass door,
       sipping coffee in my favorite rocker,
          facing your empty one at a diagonal.

Soon there will be synchronized rocking,
       front rocker blades almost touching,
          and the duet of sister language.

Family Cabin

Once revered but long neglected
The cottage suffered slow decline

For him, it was in decent shape—
I wished that someone else would buy

Mildewed towels, dank damp wood
Broken door rails, sagging shelves

Soiled couch, three stained throw pillows
Window hinges, stuck and creaking

Overhaul! Was it betrayal?
Dare I make it really mine?

Remove the dark restricting walls
Discard old heavy desk and carpets

Out with stuff, the cracked chipped china
Ditch the tired mahogany chest

Make it light, as light as light
Open kitchen, flood lamps bright

Fling round color, turquoise accents
Let the rugs sing yellow, red

I brought him in for a once-over
Fearing I had wrecked the place

He hesitated at the door
Noticed inner walls were gone

Shuffled towards the study window,
Checked to see The Tree was there

Had the bears been by this summer?
Were the wasps back under eaves?

Asked about the water heater,
Reminded us that Brett could mow

Remarked he hated basement steps
Detested cleaning chimney flues

Wished he'd thought of better lighting
Could have used it near his easel

Wheezing, leaned against the fireplace
"I love this cottage. Looks like you."

Can My Two American Homes Relate? I Eavesdrop…

A tall apartment building in the city,
Van Ness Street, Washington, DC

> *A cottage in the woods,*
> *Ragged Mountain, Andover, NH*

> They lean in for conversation
> Straining to translate

"The soot rains hard this fall
Black-tops are pot-holed and pock-marked."

> *"Heavy glass pellets drum the tin roof*
> *Mice squeeze into the basement."*

"Swimming pools are closed, umbrellas battened
Lifeguards have gone back to Romania."

> *"Cole Pond braces for the first freeze*
> *The Burnham family stacks wood."*

> A Nor'easter strikes,
> all connections fizzle out.
> Endless winter muffles both homes, til
> they find their Spring vernacular

> *"The mud won't last forever here*
> *Forsythias shower gold*
> *The stars stay late to wait for you."*

"City cranes stretch to greet your birches
Cherry blossoms burst in blush
The street lights will guide you home."

> My outlanders harmonize,
> cheering as city trucks
> roar past stoplights and

fade into the soundless
country eclipse of the moon.

Snowporch

Snow piled up Sunday
swirling on the balcony
Two wrought iron chairs
braced for the season snuggle
cloaked with puffy white armrests

I Wish I Had Asked More about Priscilla

He met her before he met my mother
Priscilla was taller than he, taller with long
bony fingers

An artist, a painter I presumed,
relaxed, looser than my mother
Low velvet voice

If born during my day, she'd be me,
pierced ears, faded jeans,
Birkenstocks

My father said she had long
wheat-colored hair—curly hair
I'm sure was unruly

I could picture her on her stool,
day-dreaming at the window, third floor
Rue de Rêves

She had pale freckles I bet,
and a thin chain bracelet, bronze,
with a charm

She probably had one brother,
wool hat pulled to his eyebrows
and they smoked Gitanes

I'm sure she wandered the Tuileries,
sitting for spells, grass underfoot,
conferring with birds

Priscilla kept her own hours,
hours that did not heed time
or daylight

I roamed the Louvre at night too
Perhaps the mauve cloche I wore
reminded Dad of her

From the High Shelf

This is not my usual flying dream,
where I push my long arms down,
feeling light under my armpits.

This time I flutter to the top
of my father's hospital closet,
stop, and take stock of his room.

He's had breakfast, brushes
crumbs off his gray pajamas,
and searches for old hearing aids.

On the rolling cart, a crimped straw
bends over his cup of water,
eggs congeal.

Thin-haired Marilyn
is his nurse today. She grumbles,
he barks, they laugh.

She remembers his father
who delivered her, and sewed
up her brother's leg.

Marilyn likes our paintings
tacked all over the walls
despite hospital rules.

She helps us go AWOL,
me pushing his wheelchair,
oxygen tubes flapping.

Racing up Main Street,
we make it to Colonial Drug,
buy four newspapers.

He checks the weekend scores,
wants to know how his
ball team is doing.

Back under covers, he's exhausted,
removes his cap with a "B,"
throws it aside.

I ask if he plans to cheer for his
"Stink Sox" tonight. In my dream,
the former shortstop nods his head.

Nursing Home in New London, NH

As any good daughter would, I visit my mother—
    open the door, notice the resident cat on the bed.

The scene is predictable: Mom propped up on pillows,
    used Kleenex at her elbow, crossword puzzle

undone at her side. Opaque eyes flicker at
    her book. She is drowsing, not reading.

She hears well—sits up abruptly as I
    come nearer. She was sharp, before the memory went,

before she chose the turquoise shirt every day, dirty or not,
    before she was placed behind locked doors.

I sit beside her— "Let's go have lunch, Mom."
    She has forgotten the time, misplaces the day.

I comb her brown-gray hair to cover the bald spot,
    spray Estee Lauder to mask the B.O.

Mother keeps her manners intact—
    perfectly precise—says all the right things,

nods at the inmates who size up her guest. She knows
    her own chair, orders grilled cheese.

Her face says *This is my daughter. From Washington.*
    Lunch is of no use. She cannot swallow.

The black cat is waiting patiently when we return.
    Nurse Anne notes he's been there three days.

He blinks slowly. Uncanny, unerring. He appears calm,
    ready to show the way.

I kiss Mom on the top of her head and leave. She
    leans back on her bed, breathing in time with the cat.

Visit to Varanasi Forty-Seven Years Later

As I find my way down a steep filthy alley, a bony cow with dung on her hind hip pushes past

My guide, Bena, waits in a wooden rowboat below, her head loosely wrapped in a light purple shawl

Two thin oarsmen row us out, bumping through clusters of boats that gather at sunset, vying for sightlines

Blazing funeral pyres dot the landing. Lopsided dwellings press against crenulated temples

Crisscrossed by swarms of electrical wires, lights throw rippling reflections, darting fingers reaching

Bena says miniature clay lamps can be set free in the black water, a holy way to bid farewell to the dead and dying

My cupped hands tremble as I lean over the side and lower them into the Ganges, one by one

The first lamp carries a candle for my father, who forms his own vanishing stream in the current

Three yellow marigolds for my mother follow swiftly, forming rivulets back and forth across his wake

Homescapes

All airports seem like home to me
       The lexicon familiar

Stacks of colored passports
       Scores of pages, crooked stamps

Vaccination booklets claim protection
       Typhus, smallpox, cholera, mumps

Traveling clothes of many styles
       Eskimo boots, salwar-kameez

Food packed in unusual wrappers
       Pakoras in plastic, peanuts in cones

Swirling words in many tongues
       "Bonjour", "Hello", "Marhaba!"

Foreign bodies walking, galloping
       Pace and gait do differ

I dream we are all family
       Each headed home somewhere

Blurry sounds from loudspeakers
       Johannesbork, and *Hamsterdam*

We all were born of the same clan
       We all share sun and moon

The tilt of a head, shape of a smile
       Linger where we meet—
       And leave again

Thanks

I am grateful to the people who made this book possible:

my sister and first reader, novelist Betsy Woodman, who has been my writing guru and co-conspirator since she was six and I was four

the magical visionaries at The Writer's Hotel and The New Guard Review: Founding Editor, Shanna McNair, and Consulting Editor, Scott Wolven

my cherished friends and writing companions, Sarah Toth and Bill Kircher, who read many versions of these poems with me

my extraordinary critics and fellow poets: Grace Cavalieri, Natwar Gandhi, Chris Bursk, Sue Ellen Thompson, Richard Blanco, and Alexandra Oliver

my steadfast supporters: Susan Clampitt, Jeremy Waletzky, Virginia Rice, Stephanie Cotsirilos, and Tanner Stening

my generous instructors from The Writer's Center in Bethesda, Maryland: Judith Harris, Meg Eden, Nan Fry, and Alexis Pope, and from Sun Magazine's annual conference, "Into the Fire": Sparrow, Heather Sellers, and Joe Wilkins

and with joy and heartfelt thanks to Leah Maines, Kevin Maines, and Christen Kincaid of Finishing Line Press.

Lee Woodman is the winner of the 2020 William Meredith Prize for Poetry. Her essays and poems have been published in *Tiferet Journal, Zócalo Public Square, Grey Sparrow Press, The Ekphrastic Review, vox poetica, The New Guard Review, The Concord Monitor, The Hill Rag,* and *Naugatuck River Review.* A Pushcart nominee, she received an Individual Poetry Fellowship from the DC Commission on the Arts and Humanities FY 2019 and FY 2020. Her poetry collection, *Mindscapes*, was published by Poets' Choice Publishing on January 9, 2020.

Woodman is a longtime artist and media producer, whose radio and film awards include five CINEs, two NY International Film Blue Ribbons, and three Gracies from American Women in Radio and Television. She worked for 20 years in leadership roles at the Smithsonian, was Vice-President of Media and Editorial at K12, Inc., and Executive Producer at Lee Woodman Media, Inc., with clients including The Library of Congress, The World Bank, Public Radio International, NPR, and the Fulbright Program.

An overseas childhood in France and India through age fourteen sparked her love for language, art, theater and dance. She now lives in Washington, DC.

CPSIA information can be obtained
at www.ICGtesting.com
Printed in the USA
FSHW020624050620
70716FS